This Journal Belongs To

_____

_____

_____

Copyright 2019 Nimble Muse Journals
All of our designs and poems are copyrighted and are not for commercial use, resell or sharing.

For spiral bound journals (personalized and non-personalized) and other products with this and other designs, please visit us at our Etsy shop.
www.nimblemuseprintables.etsy.com

For questions and/or concerns, contact us at
nimblemuse@gmail.com

If you have enjoyed this publication and found it useful, we would be grateful if you would leave us a review.
Thank you.

Made in the USA
Columbia, SC
06 May 2024

35343678R00070